Glow-in-the-Dark Animals

GLOWWORMS

Kristen Rajczak

PowerKiDS
press.

New York

Published in 2015 by The Rosen Publishing Group, Inc.
29 East 21st Street, New York, NY 10010

First Edition

Editor: Katie Kawa
Book Design: Katelyn Londino

Photo Credits: Cover Richard Packwood/Photodisc/Getty Images; cover, pp. 1–24 (background texture) olesya k/Shutterstock.com; p. 4 (inset) James Jordan Photography/Moment/Getty Images; pp. 4–5 Henrik Larsson/Shutterstock.com; pp. 6–7 http://en.wikipedia.org/wiki/Neotropic_ecozone#mediaviewer/File:Ecozone_Neotropic.svg; p. 7 (inset) Geoff Gallice/www.flickr.com/photos/dejeuxx/13676432265/CC BY 2.0; pp. 8–9, 18–19 Lyle J. Buss, Entomology & Nematology Dept., University of Florida; p. 10 (inset) Brandon Alms/Shutterstock.com; pp. 10–11, 12–13, 16–17 Robert F. Sisson/National Geographic/Getty Images; pp. 14–15 James E. Lloyd, Entomology & Nematology Dept., University of Florida; pp. 20–21 Carsten Peter/National Geographic/Getty Images; p. 22 Geoff Gallice/www.flickr.com/photos/dejeuxx/13676503245/CC BY 2.0.

Library of Congress Cataloging-in-Publication Data

Rajczak, Kristen, author.
 Glowworms / Kristen Rajczak.
     pages cm. — (Glow-in-the-dark animals)
 Includes index.
 ISBN 978-1-4994-0127-1 (pbk.)
 ISBN 978-1-4994-0129-5 (6 pack)
 ISBN 978-1-4994-0126-4 (library binding)
 1. Phenogodidae—Juvenile literature. 2. Bioluminescence—Juvenile literature. I. Title.
 QL596.P47R35 2015
 595.76'44—dc23
                                    2014028989

Manufactured in the United States of America

CPSIA Compliance Information: Batch #CW15PK: For Further Information contact Rosen Publishing, New York, New York at 1-800-237-9932

CONTENTS

What's That Glow? 4

New World Beetles. 6

Spot the Males. 8

Ladies and Larvae 10

Light Up!. 12

A Reason to Glow. 14

Early Life. 16

Glowworm Meals 18

Other Glowworms 20

Fun Glowworm Facts. 22

Glossary 23

Index. 24

Websites 24

WHAT'S THAT GLOW?

Any **insect** that gives off light and crawls along the ground may be called a glowworm. For example, you may have heard that the larvae of fireflies are called glowworms. Many insects called glowworms are types of beetle—an insect recognizable by its two pairs of wings. The front pair is large and somewhat hard, and covers the back pair, which is used for flying.

There's one kind of beetle so suited to the name "glowworm" they're called glowworm beetles! These beetles are part of the animal family Phengodidae (FEHN-goh-dih-dee). Both adults and larvae of this **species** look like worms and can light up!

firefly

Fireflies are a type of beetle, too. They produce short flashes of light, while glowworm beetles glow for longer periods of time.

NEWS FLASH!

Beetles are the most common insect on Earth.

NEW WORLD BEETLES

Glowworm beetles in the Phengodidae family are found in the Western **Hemisphere**. They live as far north as the northern United States and as far south as Chile in South America. Most of them are found in the Neotropics, which reach from Mexico to the tip of South America. The weather in this part of the world is often hot—glowworm beetles must like the heat!

So far, scientists have found more than 250 species of glowworm beetles. About 23 of these can be found in the United States. Many are most common in the southwestern part of the country.

The Neotropics, shown in green on this map, have the greatest diversity of glowworm beetles. "Diversity" means there's a wide range of many types of them.

North
America

South
America

Pacific
Ocean

Atlantic
Ocean

NEWS FLASH!

The family of insects that glowworm beetles are a part of is called a New World family. This is because European **explorers** once called the Americas the New World.

SPOT THE MALES

Since they're a kind of beetle, glowworm beetles have two sets of wings—at least the adult males do! Males have six legs and are brownish or brownish-black. Male glowworm beetles have large **mandibles** and big eyes on the sides of their head.

Adult males have a body feature that makes them easy to spot. They have two long antennae growing from their head that look like feathers or branches. Each antenna has many **segments**.

Only some species of male glowworm beetles glow. However, most males like to gather around lights when they fly at night.

Adult male glowworm beetles only grow to about 0.2 to 1.4 inches (5 to 36 mm) long, depending on the species.

LADIES AND LARVAE

Female glowworm beetles look very different from males. They don't even have wings! Female glowworms look a lot like their larvae, so their body is called larviform. They're a light brown or tan color, with black or red areas on their long, wormlike bodies. Three pairs of legs are found along their body, and each leg ends with one claw.

Can you tell adult females and larvae apart? It's hard, especially because both have the ability to glow! However, the adult females have an opening under the end of their body from which they lay eggs. They also have compound eyes, which larvae don't.

NEWS FLASH!

A compound eye is an eye made up of many separate visual units, or parts used to see.

In many species of glowing beetles, it's much more common for larvae to glow than adults.

LIGHT UP!

The glow of female glowworm beetles and their larvae is called bioluminescence (by-oh-loo-muh-NEH-suhns). "Bio" means "life," and "lumen" means "light." Bioluminescence is the light created by living things, such as glowworms. The mixing of **chemicals** inside an animal's body causes bioluminescent creatures to glow.

NEWS FLASH!

Glowworm beetles are sometimes called railroad worms, even though that's really only one kind. The spots of light on each side of the beetle's body make these insects look like train cars at night.

Female glowworm beetles and larvae have special light **organs** on each segment of their body, which look like spots of light along each side. Some also have glowing bands between their body segments. Their light is commonly a yellowish-green color and glows steadily for a while, unlike the flashes of a firefly.

The railroad worm also has a red light that glows near its head.

A REASON TO GLOW

It's cool to see glowworm beetles light up, but there's a reason for their bioluminescence. Glowworm beetles need to **protect** themselves. Their glow might be used to scare away animals that want a glowworm snack. The glow shows that they don't taste good!

Female glowworm beetles use their glow to protect their eggs, too. After laying their eggs, female glowworm beetles encircle them, glowing the whole time.

Bioluminescence plays a big role in some animals' **mating**. In the mating of glowworm beetles, the glow actually only plays a small part.

Glowworm beetles are nocturnal, or most active at night.

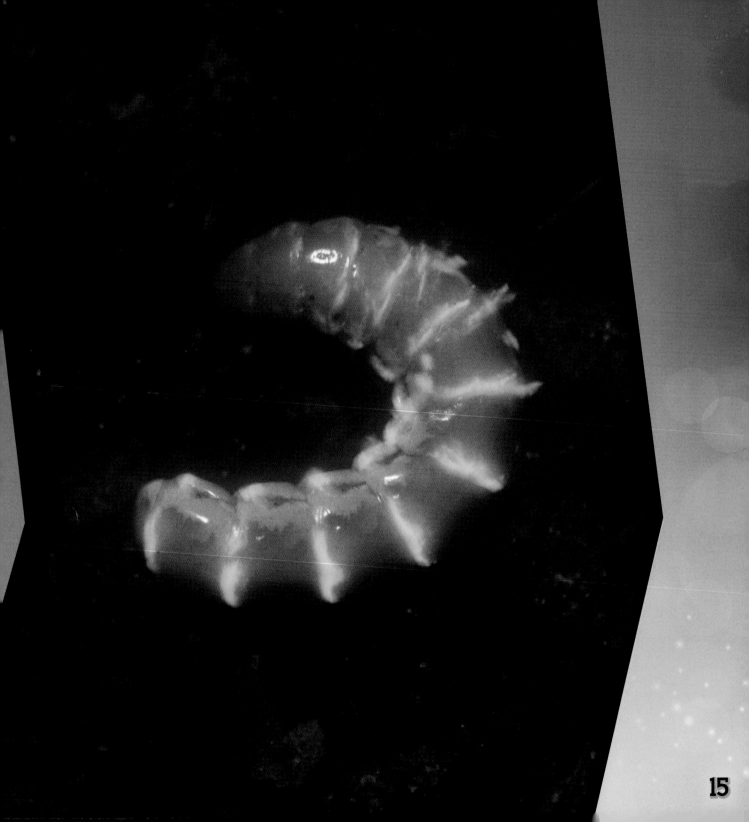

EARLY LIFE

When ready to find a mate, female glowworm beetles give off chemicals called pheromones (FEHR-uh-mohnz). In most cases, it's these—not their glow—that draw males to the females. However, once the males are close by, they might use a female's glow to find her.

A female glowworm beetle lays small eggs in a group on the ground. After about a month, the eggs glow! When the larvae come out of their eggs, they're about 0.6 to 2.5 inches (15 to 64 mm) long. They look like a worm with short legs, antennae, and very simple eyes. Glowworm larvae look a lot like adult females.

This railroad worm mother wraps her body around her eggs. She'll likely stay this way until they hatch, or come out of their eggs.

Glowing larvae are often seen in wet soil, as well as hiding under the bark or in the leaves of trees.

GLOWWORM MEALS

Only the larvae of glowworm beetles are definitely known to eat. Adult females may, but adult males aren't known to eat at all. Since they don't eat, male glowworm beetles don't live long.

Glowworm beetle larvae hunt for their favorite meal: millipedes. Once a millipede is spotted, the larva moves alongside until it can block the millipede's way with its body. Then, the larva uses its mandibles to bite the millipede and **inject** a liquid that will stop the millipede from getting away. The liquid also starts to break down the millipede's body for the larva to eat.

Once the larva bites the millipede, it buries the millipede in the ground and takes its head off! This makes it easy to crawl inside the outer shell of the millipede to eat the broken-down body.

NEWS FLASH!

Glowworm larvae crawl into
a millipede's body and eat it
from the inside!

OTHER GLOWWORMS

The common glowworm of Europe is a kind of firefly found mostly in the United Kingdom and a few other places in Europe. In this species, the larvae glow, but it's the female that glows brightest and most often. She glows when looking for a mate.

In New Zealand and Australia, the larvae of the fungus gnat are called glowworms. These larvae use their glow to draw small flying insects into sticky webs they've built. Then, they chow down! Fungus gnats are a type of fly, not a beetle, though.

The larvae of fungus gnats can make caves glow with the light from their bodies.

FUN GLOWWORM FACTS

1. While glowworm beetles are in the family Phengodidae, fireflies are beetles in the family Lampyridae (laam-PIHR-ih-dee).

2. Female glowworm beetles are larger than male glowworm beetles. They may grow to be 1.6 to 2.5 inches (41 to 64 mm) long.

3. One kind of glowworm beetle found in South America does use its glow to find a mate.

4. Scientists collect adult male glowworm beetles to study. They set up lights for them to gather around!

5. Male glowworm beetles use their many-branched antennae to track female pheromones.

6. Glowworm beetles live in burrows, or holes in the ground, during the day.

GLOSSARY

chemical: Matter that can be mixed with other matter to cause changes.

explorer: Someone who travels to find new places.

hemisphere: One-half of Earth.

inject: To use sharp teeth to force something into an animal's body.

insect: A small, often winged, animal with six legs and three body parts.

mandible: A mouthpart used to bite or hold food.

mating: Coming together to make babies.

organ: A part inside an animal's body.

protect: To keep safe.

segment: A part of a larger whole.

species: A group of plants or animals that are all the same kind.

INDEX

A

adult, 4, 8, 10, 11, 16, 18, 22

antennae, 8, 16, 22

B

bioluminescence, 12, 14

burrows, 22

E

eggs, 10, 14, 16

eyes, 8, 10, 16

F

females, 10, 12, 13, 14, 16, 18, 20, 22

fireflies, 4, 13, 20, 22

fungus gnat, 20

I

insect, 4, 5, 7, 20

L

larvae, 4, 10, 11, 12, 13, 16, 17, 18, 19, 20

light organs, 13

M

males, 8, 10, 16, 18, 22

millipedes, 18, 19

N

Neotropics, 6

P

Phengodidae, 4, 6, 22

pheromones, 16, 22

R

railroad worm, 12, 13, 16

S

species, 4, 6, 8, 11, 20

W

Western Hemisphere, 6

wings, 4, 8, 10

WEBSITES

Due to the changing nature of Internet links, PowerKids Press has developed an online list of websites related to the subject of this book. This site is updated regularly. Please use this link to access the list: www.powerkidslinks.com/gitda/glow